REDESIGN YOUR LIFE

SIMPLE STRATEGIES TO BLOOM AND LIVE A LIFE CENTERED IN CHRIST

WENDY BRYANT

Dedication

To the ones that deep in their souls know there is more to life and want to discover the fullness of it!

To Austin, Sean, Hollie, Taylor, Grace, Caleb, and Christian—I love you more than you could ever know! To the rest of my family, friends, students and customers—I'm forever grateful for you all. My prayer is that you will discover the depths of God's love to the fullest.

Table of Contents

Disclaimer

The contents of Redesign Your Life are for informational purposes only. The content is not intended to be a substitute for professional medical advice, diagnosis, or treatment. The reader should regularly consult a physician or professional licensed counselor in matters relating to his/her physical or mental health and particularly with respect to any symptoms that may require diagnosis or medical attention.

INTRODUCTION

Begin Again

*"Behold, I am doing a new thing; now it springs forth,
do you not perceive it? I will make a way in the
wilderness and rivers in the desert."*

Isaiah 43:19 (ESV)

Welcome to your divine restart. If you are like me, you have been through something. You have endured much. You have longed for a way out of the mess, a way over the mountain, a way through the pain. If you are honest, you might even wish you could go back and simply get a second chance to do life again. A redo. I know that was the cry of my heart. A cry, I feared, would never be realized.

Even though I did not crack the code of time travel, I did find a way to begin again. I have come to realize that my journey to rebirth is a gift meant to be shared with others. I am not a professional writer, I am not a counselor, and I am not a motivational speaker. I am simply a woman, just like you, with a mixed past of good memories mingled with deep hurt. I am a woman just like you, who found a pathway of purpose though the pain. I am a child of God, just like you, who discovered the secret to a redesigned life. I am compelled to share my story with you because I know that what God did for me, He will also do for you.

God wants to reveal everything to those who believe. He wants us to seek him so he can do so. God is looking for a willing heart that wants him above everything else. Are you ready for your divine restart? Are you ready to dream and hope again? Are you ready to experience true joy? Lasting peace? Unshakable freedom?

I am here to tell you that you do not have to accept a life full of depression, broken relationships, mental illness, sickness, anxiety, poverty, weariness, fear, and insignificance. Somewhere along the way, you may have accepted these conditions as truths that cannot be escaped. I used to think the same thing. But my journey with Christ has shown me the *real* truth concerning these facts is that our stories do not have to end the same way they began. The believer in Christ has access to the mind of Christ. Transformation has always been an inside-out job. It starts with your thought life. The Christ in you wants to empower you to live a life of freedom.

> **"Therefore, if anyone is in Christ, he is a new creation; old things have passed away; behold, all things have become new."**
> **2 Corinthians 5:17 (NKJV)**

In fact, God offers you more than just an upgrade—He offers you a new life. He says that those who are in Him actually become a new being. In Christ you have an invitation into a literal rebirth. "Therefore, if anyone is in Christ, he is a new creation; old things have passed away; behold, all things have become new." 2 Corinthians 5:17 (NKJV)

One day when I was praying God told me His Word was like an Easter Egg Hunt—there were treasures throughout it, and those who would seek would find! These treasures are the secrets to living a life of peace with God even in an impossible situation. God wants to reveal everything to those who believe—He wants us to seek him so he can reveal these things to us. God is looking for a willing heart that wants him above everything else. In the following pages I will show you how I found Christ in the middle of chaos.

If so, I invite you to keep reading and find Christ in the middle of the chaos. Each chapter will end with a tip so you can get the most out of this book; it will be an interactive experience. Grab a journal, a hot drink, and come join me for a transformational journey from "old" to "new."

Action Steps: Practice Stillness

- ✓ Find a quiet place where you can meet up with God daily, away from any distractions.

- ✓ Try to shut out the noise around you and practice stillness. God says, "Be still and know that I am God."

- ✓ Find some paper and a pen and begin to journal everything God tells you throughout this journey of redesigning your life with Christ.

CHAPTER 1

Lord, I Need You

Have you ever heard a song that spoke straight into your heart? I remember one such song that spoke to me so profoundly, I concluded it could only be God speaking. It was a lazy summer day, and I ran across a song by Matt Maher called "Lord, I need You." I started listening and before I knew it, a river of healing tears flowed forth from my eyes. I must have listened to the song thirty times that day, if not more, and every day for months. Little did I know the tears I cried were actually a plea to know more of God. Those four small words, "Lord, I need you," began the fresh start I had been looking for. God heard my pleading and came to my rescue!

God came to my rescue in so many ways that year. He sent friends to speak life into me through online classes I taught. He also sent a dear friend by the name of Dionne to walk alongside me and pour into me. "In my distress I called to the Lord; I called out to my God. From his temple he heard my voice; my cry came to his ears." Psalm 18:6 NIV

> **"In my distress I called to the Lord; I called out to my God. From his temple he heard my voice; my cry came to his ears." Psalm 18:6 NIV**

Just as God heard my heart cry, He will hear yours. The fresh start you are looking for may only be one heart cry away. Recognize there is a difference between a heart cry and a simple, quiet prayer. If you are ready to see real change in your life, I encourage you to cry out to God like never before. Be real. Be raw. Show up just as you are and watch the God of miracles come crashing in.

God knows what you need, and He knows who you need. God is limitless in His resources and will go through every measure to bring you into His kingdom. Let Him rescue you today! Cry out, "Abba Father, help!" When we acknowledge our need for God, His grace begins to show up to super-

> **"In all your ways acknowledge Him and He will make your paths straight." Proverbs 3:6 (NASB)**

naturally heal our hearts and change our circumstances. "In all your ways acknowledge Him and He will make your paths straight." Proverbs 3:6 (NASB)

Surrender

God's grace empowered change in me, but my surrender was the key to walking in freedom. It is not always easy to surrender in the midst of chaos, but I believe it is a posture we need to be in to experience breakthrough. I learned that in order for God to work things out for good in my life, I would continually have to trust and surrender everything to him.

One way I practice ongoing surrender is daily asking God to search my heart and reveal anything tripping me up. When I respond and repent, I know breakthrough will come. It is my desire for you to find God's endless love as you walk in the surrendered life. You will not have to walk it alone. God says He will never leave or forsake you.

Faith

If you are like me, you might associate faith with how you feel or by what you see in your physical reality, but faith is believing *before* seeing. Over this past year, I have learned to trust God even when I cannot see what lies ahead. Remember: We cannot have faith and fear at the same time. We must choose one or the other.

I have learned I can walk in peace even in the middle of a major life transition. In my natural circumstances, it may seem very overwhelming, but with faith, I can find peace in the midst of it. You still have to journey through it, but you can do it with God's grace and peace. If you are walking with God daily, He will build your faith to prepare you for what is to come. "Now faith is the substance of things hoped for, the evidence of things unseen." "And without faith it is impossible to please God, because anyone who comes to Him must believe that He exists and that He rewards those who earnestly seek Him." Hebrews 11:1 and 11:6 (NIV)

When I look back over these last two years, I can see how God was preparing me for today. He was building my faith in Him so I would trust Him without seeing. I finished writing this book before the COVID-19 pandemic hit, but I placed it up on the shelf because it still needed a deep edit. If this pandemic had hit two years ago, I would not have been strong enough to walk in faith through this traumatic event without living in fear every day. Instead, I am proud to say fear never entered my mind, and peace like a river came flooding in. I stood strong in my faith and encouraged others to lean on God's promises recorded in Psalm 91. God taught me I could trust Him no matter whatever life threw at me.

Over time, God has provided different Scripture passages to help build my faith. One such Scripture was Hebrews 11:11, which says, "By faith Sarah herself also received strength to conceive seed, and she bore a child when she was past the age, because she judged Him faithful who had promised," (NKJV).

When I read this, the words that jumped off the page at me were, "…because she JUDGED HIM FAITHFUL," (emphasis mine). It was like a lightbulb went off in my head. The exciting thing is, God is always faithful to His Word. I invite you to trust God like I did this past year–judge Him faithful. You can do what I did: I stood in the middle of difficult circumstances and did not waver. I was facing some challenges in my life, but when I read that Scripture, I decided I would judge God faithful to His Word. When I did, everything changed for the better. I learned things shift for good in our life according to our faith.

When we have faith, we do not have to wonder if everything will be okay. We know it will because God is faithful to His Word. We have to believe. I challenge you to believe today and take your life with God to a whole new level. You, too, can live a victorious, faith-filled life with Christ at the center. As you walk with God through this faith journey, ask God to reveal some areas of your life in which He wants you to have greater faith. Ask God to give you Scriptures that will open your eyes so your faith will be strengthened.

Yes, it is scary sometimes, but the more I walk by faith, the less difficult it becomes. You can strengthen your faith by choosing to believe *no matter what things look like around you.*

Action Steps: Cry Out–Surrender–Faith

- ✓ Get in a quiet place to pray.

- ✓ First, acknowledge you need God by crying out to Him for help. Hebrews 5:7 says that while Jesus was on earth, He offered prayers and pleadings, with a loud cry and tears to God. The Father heard Jesus' prayers because of His deep reverence for God. You can also pray this way!

- ✓ Pray out loud because there is just something about it. I have found that loud bold prayers are powerful when breakthrough is needed. If you are reading this and cannot pray loudly, then it is okay to just pray it. God will hear and send an army of angels like He did for me.

- ✓ Ask God to reveal the areas of your life where you need to have faith. Surrender whatever God reveals to you. Journal everything, because one day when you look back, you will be able to see how much you have grown.

CHAPTER 2

An Experiential God

I used to think God was just sitting up in Heaven watching our every mistake, waiting to punish us for doing wrong. Thank goodness God sends people across our path to help us on our journey. Through an online webinar for The Thriving Christian Artist, God introduced me to someone named Matt Tommey. God used Matt's teaching style to reach my heart, and I began to understand God was not sitting around waiting to catch me doing something wrong. Matt helped me see how God is a God of forgiveness—He in fact not only forgives our sin but remembers it no more! I learned God wanted to have a relationship with me. He wanted to talk with me and dream with me! God was not angry and distant as I had supposed but was a God with whom I could relate. I could actually communicate with Him! How exciting is that? A God who wants to communicate with me!

This should not have been new news to me. I mean, I had heard the Gospel on and off throughout my entire life. As a young child, I rode the bus to church weekly. When my boys were growing up, I was at church every time the doors were open. I taught Sunday School, worked in the nursery, and did visitation on Wednesday nights. But somehow, I missed this loving and forgiving God that I now know–the God who wants to have this relationship with me.

How did I miss this? Was it because I did not study my Bible enough, or maybe because I did not pray hard enough? No, I do not think it was any of these. I honestly believe I was lacking some powerful keys about what it meant to be in relationship with God. I did not understand the power or practicalities behind the idea of worshipping God in Spirit and in Truth, and I really had no idea what it meant to be led by the Holy Spirit. Gaining an understanding on these two key ideas transformed my relationship with Jesus.

This transformation occurred not only by revelation, but also by activation. It happened for me when I put action behind what I was learning. I started asking for eyes to see and ears to hear. This really opened up the communication channels between God and me. It changed how I viewed God, others, and even myself. I began to see and feel through God's eyes and heart. As this happened, I could sense my heart changing, and I loved the new me. I was no longer angry at the world because of past hurts.

God will meet you where you are, so you do not have to have it all figured it out. God knows you and He knows the desires of your heart. If your desire is to know God in a deeper way, then pray for that. Ask God to strengthen your desire for Him. Because God knows your unspoken motives (and there is a difference between questioning God and asking questions), you do not ever need to be afraid to ask God questions. Taste and see that He is good!

Worship Is One Way of Tasting

For me, the best way to begin praying is by sitting still and worshiping God. I like to worship in song and then transition into worshipping with words of thanksgiving to the Father. Most days, I just sing a song from my heart, but sometimes I will find a song online and start there. It may take a few minutes or longer to feel God's presence while worshipping—I just keep going until I can feel Him present in the room. If I had to describe this presence, I would say it is a weightiness combined with a sense of awe. Sometimes I feel emotions well up inside me, a sense of gratitude in my heart. If you are new to worshipping, this process could take longer, so do not be discouraged. I remember not feeling much when I first began these practices. Even still, over the past year I learned that worship brings so much joy, peace, and breakthrough in my life. "Worship in awe and wonder, all you who've been made holy! For all who fear Him will feast with plenty. Even the strong and the wealthy grow weak and hungry, but those who passionately pursue the Lord will never lack any good thing." Psalm 34:9-10 (TPT)

James 4:8 says it something like this: The closer you draw to the Lord, the closer He draws to you. This past year, I witnessed that Scripture firsthand. I know the same will be true of you also as you start drawing near to God. "My friend, it really is that simple," God whispered in my ear, so many times over this past year. He would often tell me to keep it simple—like a child. "Have the faith of a child, Wendy. Don't overthink things."

Lately, Visions in Worship has become a common occurrence for me. Do not be surprised if God starts giving you visions during your worship time! The other day during worship, God showed me a glimpse of Heaven! I was wondering about my mom, just missing her, and talking to God about her. He showed me her in heaven amongst thousands of people with their hands raised, singing praises to Him. Everything was glowing in the light of His presence! It was a beautiful sight to behold! I want to encourage you to open your mouth and release your sound in worship–Praise Him for He is good.

Experience Breakthrough in Your Worship

"What is breakthrough, and how can I get it?", you might ask. It might mean you need to break out of a certain mindset. It might be a breakthrough in your business or healing from an illness. What do you need breakthrough in today? So much of my breakthrough happened while in worship, because things start to shift as we worship God. I always leave so refreshed, full of joy and with a new perspective on life or a specific situation. Worshipping for me is like oxygen—without it I cannot survive. Something wonderful happens in the worship that is indescribable. I believe this is what was missing in my walk with God so many years ago. Without worship, we stay defeated and depleted of what we need—instead of living the abundant life, we barely survive. Worship breaks off the strongholds of depression, broken relationships, mental illness, sickness, anxiety, poverty, weariness, fear, and insignificance. I know you will discover the power of worship like I did!

Worship first, because worship brings breakthrough, and Faith pleases God. I can't say it any better than Tommy Walker said it in an article about his life: "When we worship, the invisible God is at work doing invisible and powerful things. We get realigned, refreshed, and refueled; we find unspeakable joy and indescribable peace. We discover the breakthrough strength of God, which enables us to walk in the truth, live in His presence and see Him fight our battles for us. It is how we can put the beauty of the Gospel on display, receive His many blessings and at the same time be a blessing to the world."

Breakthrough also happens in prayer. In Matthew 7, we learn that if we pray and keep on asking and knocking, then the door will be opened. Everyone who seeks finds. In Matthew 7:7-8 (NIV), it says, "Keep on asking and you will receive what you ask for. Keep on seeking, and you will find. Keep on knocking and the door will be opened to you. For everyone who seeks receives. Everyone who seeks finds. And to everyone who knocks, the door will be opened." We should not grow weary in our asking and praying. God promises that if we keep seeking and asking then we will find, and the door will be opened. I do not know about you, but this is exciting. I have learned to stand in this verse, even reminding God of this verse sometimes when I am praying.

One approach is to pray a Bible verse just by saying it a little differently, changing the wording to fit whatever you are facing. I learned this from a beautiful woman of faith by the name of Karen Wheaton, who shares from her heart through videos about her prodigal daughter.

I might say something like this: "God, it's Wendy, and I'm standing at the door knocking. My heart is broken, and my current situation does not look so good. Father, You tell us in Matthew 7:7-8 if we knock then the door will be opened. Thank You, Father, that this door will be opened according to Your will, and You will reveal to me all I need to know to get out of this situation. God, You say everyone who seeks finds. I am seeking answers on how to move forward and which way I should go. Thank you, Father, that the answer to what I am seeking is found in You. You also say if we ask, we will receive.

Father, today I am asking for a way out because You tell us in Your Word that You always provide a way out. Thank you, Father, that Your Word is alive today and never changes. I ask all these things in Jesus' name. Amen."

Sometimes, we just need to decree or declare to see breakthrough. I once heard someone say, "We need to know when to pray and when to decree. When the tornado is coming toward your home, it is not time to pray. It is time to decree. Speak to it and tell it to dissolve or to go around your home."

"Truly I tell you, if anyone says to this mountain, Go, throw yourself into the sea, 'and does not doubt in their heart but believes that what they say will happen, it will be done for them." Mark 11:23 (NIV)

That changed my perspective on a lot of things. If we do not see mountains move, maybe it is because we are praying when we should be decreeing and telling the mountain to move! We have to act and use God's words as a weapon! "Truly I tell you, if anyone says to this mountain, Go, throw yourself into the sea, 'and does not doubt in their heart but believes that what they say will happen, it will be done for them." Mark 11:23 (NIV)

God says we can tell the mountain to move and it will if we believe it in our hearts. The key, my friend, is believing! The mountain will move when you plant your feet in Jesus and do not sway. Over this past year, I have had a lot of opportunities to tell the mountain to move. While helping a family member walk through a rough spot, I noticed things shifting—mountains moving in a mighty way. I set my mind on Jesus and followed the Holy Spirit's voice throughout that time. When we won a court case, the attorney looked at us and said, "Honestly, I wasn't sure we would win." I just smiled and said, "I never doubted it."

What mountain are you facing today that looks way too big? With Jesus on your side, you are sure to win. Plant your feet like I did and believe His promises. Watch and be expectant as you wait for the victory!

Holy Spirit

Romans 15:13 (NIV) says, "May the God of hope fill you with all joy and peace as you trust him, so that you may overflow with hope by the power of the Holy Spirit." I do not believe we can taste all of God's goodness without the Holy Spirit dwelling within us. From my experience, it is the Holy Spirit in us that guides us and fills our cup to overflowing like the Scripture above says—so that we may overflow with HOPE by the power of the Holy Spirit.

Earlier in the same letter, Scripture says, "And hope does not put us to shame, because God's love has been poured out into our hearts through the Holy Spirit, who has been given to us," (Romans 5:5, NIV). The Holy Spirit transforms you so you can live a victorious life in Christ. Transformation happens when you surrender to Jesus and allow the Holy Spirit to guide you.

I remember being baptized, and they said, "I'm baptizing you in the name of The Father, The Son, and Holy Spirit." I really never thought much more about that until these last few years when I came to know the Holy Spirit in a powerful way. I believe there is a difference in being baptized "in the name of" and being baptized "by" the Holy Spirit—at least for me there was a major difference. You might ask, "How do I get baptized by the Holy Spirit?" Well, I thought you would never ask!

I just kept knocking, asking, and seeking. I would invite the Holy Spirit into my day, my prayer time, and my creative time. Honestly, at first nothing seemed different, but slowly I could feel things shifting. I started having visions and dreams, and I could hear Gods voice. Joy took over my life and my smiles were real–not fake. No more anxiety; all fear was gone.

Just imagine life with joy and no fear. I remember asking the Holy Spirit to bubble in and out of me and into other people's lives. I am so happy to say it is happening. Something I never thought would be is now a reality. You, too, will have this as you keep knocking and seeking God. "But you will receive power when the Holy Spirit comes on you; and you will be my witnesses in Jerusalem, and in Judea and Samaria, and to the ends of the earth." Acts 1:8 (NIV)

> **"But you will receive power when the Holy Spirit comes on you; and you will be my witnesses in Jerusalem, and in Judea and Samaria, and to the ends of the earth."**
> **Acts 1:8 (NIV)**

We must seek God daily through worship, time in the secret place, and in His Word. The more we let Jesus' light shine in us, the less room remains for darkness, and then the transformation starts to happen. God's Word is powerful to transform us as we allow the Holy Spirit to reveal and guide us. God's Word is alive and powerful. As we believe and receive God's Word, we are ultimately receiving life! As my friend, Dionne, would say, "Eat the Word." How do we eat the Word? We read God's Word daily and let the Holy Spirit bring revelation so we can understand and start applying it to our life! You may be like I once was: I would read the Bible, but nothing really made a lot of sense. I would read it anyway, hoping to find the secrets to the joyful and peaceful life I heard the preacher talk about from the pulpit. Here is a secret: It goes deeper than that! We need the Holy Spirit alive and working in us so we can have a deeper understanding of the Bible. Ask the Holy Spirit to reveal God's Word in a deeper way. Ask God to give you fresh eyes to see and to understand with. I am no expert on all the teachings of the Holy Spirit, but the one thing I do know is that He will lead you in the way God wants you to go.

Action Steps: Worship–Prayer–Decree

- ✓ Pray and ask God to open the eyes of your heart, to give you a heart like His, and to give you ears to hear. This simple prayer will start to transform your heart and mind in ways you never thought possible.

- ✓ Worship God daily, for at least 15 minutes. Worship opens up the doors of heaven.

- ✓ Seek to know the Holy Spirit in a new way—invite Him into your life daily. Read these Scriptures: 1 Corinthians 2:10, John 14:26, Acts 2:4, Acts 2:38.

- ✓ Tell the mountains in your life to move.

CHAPTER 3

Leave the Past Behind

As a teenager I decided to pull my bootstraps up, leave the past behind, and go after my future. I grew up and thought I would not ever have to look back. I did not know it then, but my past had a tight hold on me. One day, God reminded me of some things from my past. I was surprised. He told me I needed to revisit these things *with Him* so I could get the healing I needed to move into the fullness of what my future held.

My mother struggled with mental illness. Because of this, I spent many nights afraid of what might happen and of what she might do. Later in my mom's life, she decided to journal. As I was beginning to process my past with God's help, He reminded me of her journals, which I had not thought about since her death 21 years earlier. I asked God if He wanted me to go through them. He whispered, "There is wisdom and understanding in them." I called my sister to ask about the journals, but I could tell she was a little hesitant to share them with me. I am sure she was worried how it might affect me. Still, she agreed.

As I started reading, I noticed a pattern. My mom faithfully journaled almost every day, and every entry was addressed to Abba Father! She started each with praise and thanksgiving! The letters also revealed how God faithfully provided for her when she was a single woman in her late-40s to mid-50s. I am very thankful that God brought these journals to my memory, because I now understand things about my mom I would not have known otherwise. I now know how she made peace with God and relied on Him for everything. She wrote about how He comforted her daily. This knowledge became another steppingstone, to help me climb over another obstacle and bust through a wall that was holding me back without me even realizing it.

As a teenager, I had put up a wall to protect myself. But over the last few years, I have learned to let go of things that were hindering my walk with God. All the baggage had to go. I often refer to my old self as being "buried alive." There was so much weight on me that I felt as if I was suffocating on most days.

What walls have you built for protection that need to come down? They may have been needed at one time, but now they are blocking good things. Ask God to reveal them to you.

When you clean your heart and mind, you create space for God to start working in your life. It gives God room to replace the old with new! Just like when you clean and declutter your home, you create space for new things or make more breathing room. It is so much easier to maintain this if you do it often. In your home, the clutter will stay under control. In your relationship with God, it helps you to keep your eyes focused on Jesus.

Renew Your Mind

I was recently listening to a speech by Bishop T.D. Jakes, and he said something that jumped out at me. "When you hold onto your history, you do it at the expense of your destiny." Wow, this is so powerful and true! If you keep holding on to past hurts and lies, how can God move forward in your life?

Do you ever wonder why you are mentally exhausted? It could be because you are holding on to hurt and lies from the past, keeping God from moving forward in your life. Let go of the old things that are holding you back and a new freedom and energy will come. God loves to replace the old with the new! Let Him plant the seeds of tomorrow so you can have a beautiful garden soon!

One of my favorite things to do is to create new pieces of clothing from fabric and clothing others have discarded because they do not see a purpose in it anymore. I often relate this to our inner lives—a lot of times, you may have thoughts that clutter your mind. Perhaps you hold on to thoughts of worthlessness and shame, or perhaps you feel discarded by so many. When you allow bad thoughts to linger in your mind, it starts to get cluttered. When this happens, you have no clarity, you cannot think straight, and you do not always make the best choices. Your thoughts are the blueprints of your life, and you need to clear out those thoughts! Let go of them and allow God to show you who you are in Him. When He does, you can replace those thoughts with good! **So, clear your mind by asking God to show you thoughts you need to let go of.** Ask God to change and replace old thoughts with new thoughts! Allow God to redesign your life with new

> **Do not conform to the pattern of this world, but be transformed by the renewing of your mind. Then you will be able to test and approve what God's will is—his good, pleasing, and perfect will." Romans 12:2 (NIV)**

blueprints! Do not conform to the pattern of this world, but be transformed by the renewing of your mind. Then you will be able to test and approve what God's will is-his good, pleasing, and perfect will." Romans 12:2 (NIV)

We can renew our minds through worship and prayer, as we discussed in earlier chapters. We can also renew our minds by reading God's Word, laying things at His feet, listening for His voice, and conversing with other like-minded believers. Listen for God's voice throughout your day—let it guide you. To me, God's voice is a still, small voice in the back of my mind. It is always encouraging, and it never tears me down. God always speaks out of love. I love this verse in Isaiah 26:3: "You keep him in perfect peace whose mind is stayed on you, because he trusts in you." When our minds are focused on God and we trust Him, then we have perfect peace!

Remember, your past does not determine your future. Yes, your past experiences had to happen to help you become who you are today, but that doesn't mean you are the same person you were when you started those chapters of your life! Every experience can teach us something or bring us to a better place. Think about it: God brought you through to make you stronger, not to stay in the past. Shake it off. Release it so you can walk into what God has for you! Walk like you have been through something, with your back a little straighter and your step a little lighter. Move in confidence knowing God is leading the way–He is your light!

Forgive

Forgiveness is another powerful tool in the journey to leave baggage from our past behind–we must learn to forgive others and ourselves. When we do this, we allow love to come crashing in. Forgiveness has nothing to do with excusing someone's behavior or saying what they did to you was okay. It does not mean you were wrong, or they were right. Rather, forgiveness is necessary so you can get passed the anger and hurt and open your heart up to new possibilities God has for you. You must forgive to move on. If you do not forgive, then you will stay angry and unable to really experience all of God's love. Holding on to anger closes you off from new possibilities, because all your energy is wrapped around being angry. You think about it often and play it out in your head over and over. If you are unsure if anger is holding you captive, try the anger test: When you think of that incident or person, do you feel your blood pressure rising or feel overwhelmed? Do you start replaying past circumstances and interactions in your head and get mad? If so, you are angry! Bring the person or situation to God, lay it at His feet, and forgive.

Replace with Good

It is not enough to just let go. Once you let go of things, remember to ask God to replace them with good! This is where God really starts to move; this process was like gold for me. I get so excited when I speak about this! Ask God to replace the bad, and then step back and watch as God starts bringing good in your life. Your life will start to change in ways you never thought possible. All the seeds of good that God is planting will bring a huge harvest. This is why this process is so important! You want your life to have a continuous harvest as you continue evolving into who God wants you to be! The harvest will depend on how much you let go of and ask God to replace with good. Stop holding on to old thoughts, sins, hurts, excuses and so on. Let go of it all—lay it at His feet! Trust Him alone, step out in faith.

Action Steps:

- ✓ Do not be afraid to revisit your past with God as your helper. Pray, and ask God to reveal what from your past might be holding you back.

- ✓ Ask yourself, "Who do I need to forgive today? What do I need to forgive myself for today?" Pray for those situations and lay them at God's feet.

- ✓ Renew your mind through practices of worship, prayer, being with other believers, and listening for God's voice.

- ✓ As you let go of burdens from the past, ask God to replace the bad with good.

- ✓ As you pray and practice forgiveness, journal everything that God tells you.

CHAPTER 4

Who Am I in Christ?

"Now if anyone is enfolded into Christ. He has become an entirely new creation. All that is related to the old order has vanished. Behold, everything is fresh and new."

2 Corinthians 5:16 (TPT)

For most of my life, I carried a particular frustration with me. It is hard to explain, but maybe you have felt it also. I always felt an urge to create. It was an overwhelming desire in my head that just would not go away, like I was created for more but did not know how to find it. At one point in my life, I put away the art, hoping this nagging desire would go away. To me, it truly felt like a nagging rather than a longing, because creativity seemed to interfere with what I thought life was supposed to be. Back then, I never asked God what He had planned for my life. I just believed what I saw and heard instead of consulting the One who created me. Honestly, I did not know the Father would even communicate with me on this level.

My thoughts on life went like this: You get married, have a family, and just enjoy life. Be satisfied with what God gave you. But it was never enough; I never felt satisfied in life unless I was creating, but creating seemed to get in the way of these other things. So, I always felt frustrated, never satisfied, and angry when I was not creating. That feeling never went away, calling me to create. At one point in my life, I said it was a curse. I never really told anyone about how I felt. I kept it bottled up inside of me, ashamed of these feelings and questions. I tried everything to make these feelings go away, but nothing satisfied the nagging. This is because the only one who can satisfy this is God. I always felt like something was wrong with me, I was different, I did not fit in—there was this restlessness inside of me that needed to be channeled, even as a child.

I did not understand that creating could be the thing that grounded me and allowed me to come into wholeness. Today, I am happy to say God has changed my heart about this. I have learned to channel my calling to create with God. I now know it was God calling me to Him; creating became a time of worship, and a time to spend dreaming and planning with God.

"Who am I Lord? For what purpose was I created?" I challenge you to ask God these questions because when you do, I think you will be pleasantly surprised by His answers! The answers I got actually made me cry. I had never looked at myself the way God sees me. The old has vanished and everything is fresh and new! God tells us everything is new when Christ lives in us. If you know Christ lives in you but you do not feel new, then it is time to let go of the past and accept the gift of the new! Are you going to live life from a wounded perspective or from God's view? Tune your ear to the Holy Spirit and let Him redesign your life!

Why Was I Created?

I quickly learned that I was holding myself captive, not God. God was intentional and paid attention to every detail when creating the world! God knows every emotion, thought, and concern we have. He chose the color of your skin, the texture of your hair and the shape of your body! He gave you your personality and the talents that you have! He was intentional—it was not by mistake. God knows your value and wants you to know it also. Psalm 139:14 tells us that we praise God because we are fearfully and wonderfully made.

If you are like me then you grew up listening to so many other voices that scream you are not good enough, you are too this or too that. The problem is you start to believe these things as if they are true. God created you in the image of Christ and because of this, you are unique and special in the Father's eyes. He created you for a purpose, and when you discover and step into this purpose, you will truly shine. Throw off the lies of the enemy and start believing who Christ says you are. Recognize your value in Christ.

God says I am:

- ✓ Beloved—Jeremiah 31:3

- ✓ Child of God—1 John 3:1

- ✓ Rejoiced Over—Zephaniah 3:17

- ✓ Forgiven—1 Peter 2:24

- ✓ Washed Clean—Isaiah 1:18

- ✓ A Temple of the Holy Spirit—1 Corinthians 6:19

- ✓ Adopted into God's Family—Romans 8:15

✓ Co-Heir with Christ—Romans 8:17

✓ Righteous—2 Corinthians 5:21

✓ A New Creation in Christ—2 Corinthians 5:17

✓ A Sweet Aroma—2 Corinthians 2:15

✓ Never Alone—Deuteronomy 31:8

✓ A Masterpiece—Ephesians 2:10

✓ Set Apart—1 Peter 2:9

✓ A Co-Laborer—1 Corinthians 3:9

✓ An Ambassador of Christ—2 Corinthians 5:20

✓ Wonderfully Made—Psalm 139:14

✓ Whole in Christ—Colossians 2:10

✓ Chosen and appointed to bear fruit—John 15:16

✓ Free—Galatians 5:1

✓ Strengthened by Christ—Philippians 4:13

✓ Victorious—Psalm 18:35

✓ Bold—2 Corinthians 3:12

✓ Of a sound mind—2 Timothy 1:7

✓ A Friend of Christ—John 15:15

✓ The salt and life of the earth—Matthew 5:13-14

I am not sure who you are, but I know you were created for more than just existing. Whether you are a grandma taking care of your grandchildren or the president of a large company, remember God has a plan for your life! Be present and do it all with enthusiasm for Christ! When you start leaning into God and asking Him the tough questions, He will start revealing His plan for your life. Sometimes, He will totally change your course. Be ready and willing; step out in faith!

I pray this would be your prayer today. "Father, open my eyes to who You say I am. I want to know who I am in You—not who the world says I am. I know You created me for more. Show me what that more looks like and feels like! Father, expose the lies of the enemy and cutoff the source so I can hear Your voice. Forgive me for believing these lies. Silence the noise around me—I need to hear You today! In Jesus' name I pray, Amen." He who has an ear, let him hear what the Spirit says to the churches. To him who overcomes, to him I will give some of the hidden manna, and I will give him a white stone, and a new name written on the stone which no one knows but he who receives it." Revelation 2:17 (ESV)

He who has an ear, let him hear what the Spirit says to the churches. To him who overcomes, to him I will give some of the hidden manna, and I will give him a white stone, and a new name written on the stone which no one knows but he who receives it." Revelation 2:17 (ESV)

Action Steps:

- ✓ In prayer or journaling, take some time to ask the following questions. "Lord, who do you say I am in Christ? What name do you call me? What is in my hands today?"

- ✓ Revisit these questions frequently. The answers may change in different seasons of life.

- ✓ When the enemy rises up against you, return to these answers to remember who God says you are!

- ✓ When you know what you are called to, do not hesitate to step into that calling. Trust that God will help fit these things into your life.

- ✓ Journal everything God tells you.

CHAPTER 5

Seek and You Will Find

If you knew there were hidden treasures in your yard, would you seek them out? Last year God told me to cultivate the garden of my heart because there were treasures in it to discover. The question remained: What kind of treasures would I find?

Scripture tells us what kinds of treasures are available to us when we are seeking God:

- ✓ Strength. *Come all who are weary—come to the banquet table and feast.*

- ✓ Endurance. *For He is good, and his mercy endures forever.*

- ✓ Illumination. *His light will shine upon you to illuminate your path.*

- ✓ Breakthrough. *He will part the sea for you and make a way in the wilderness.*

✓ Hope. *You will not faint. He will mount you up on eagles' wings.*

✓ Help. *His Angels will camp near your tent.*

✓ Sustenance. *Come to Him and drink from the cup of the living water and thirst no more. You shall not want for anything, because in Him is everything.*

Like any treasure, these gifts are not at the surface for us to stumble upon. They must be sought out. The dig is worth it because the rewards are great. In fact, my treasure hunt with God has been the greatest pursuit of my life! I love discovering all the treasures in the garden God is cultivating within me. How do we uncover the treasures He has placed within us? The key lies in many of the habits and practices we have already talked about: Reading His Word, praying, worshiping, and gleaning from the wisdom of others.

But most importantly, you must remember that in order to find all the treasure God has to offer, you have to seek Him with your whole heart–you have to be all in. You get what you put into the seeking. The more you seek, the more you will find the hidden treasures. God will take you from treasure to treasure or as some would say, from glory to glory. Each treasure will lead to you wanting more of the goodness of God. I am always in awe of the goodness of God. He wants us to experience the abundant life he promises through Christ Jesus. Jesus died so we could have an abundant life, rather than a defeated life.

In many ways, my life was defined by worry and lack before I began making more time for fellowship with God. That life of worry and lack will be no more when we seek Him first. This might mean, for example, not binging on Netflix or spending all evening online. The rewards you get by spending time with the Father will far outweigh the benefits of Netflix and the Internet. I love what Psalm 34:8 says: "Taste and see that the Lord is good; blessed is the one that takes refuge in him." God says the ones who take refuge in Him are blessed! So first seek God and let Him be your refuge. What is refuge? A place of shelter! If you keep seeking and pressing in, you will find Him, and in Him is perfect love. Just keep digging and you will experience all that God has to offer soon!

One of the first things to realize as you seek God is to understand God wants you to fellowship with him–to make time for Him–because it is key to growing in intimacy and relationship. Our lives are so busy, we rarely sit and spend time with our loved ones, much less God. When God began transforming my life, I grew so hungry for Him and determined to find Him. I knew the void in my life could only be filled by him. Since that time, I have witnessed the transformation in my own life.

How many times have we tried what the world had to offer but only to be disappointed? God never disappoints. Everything else will fall into place if we learn to seek Him first! God will pour out his glory and treasure to whoever is hungry for his presence. Ultimately, the true treasure to be found is God Himself.

> "And those who know your name will put their trust in You, for You, O Lord have not forsaken those who seek You."
> Psalm 9:10 (ESV)

"And those who know your name will put their trust in You, for You, O Lord have not forsaken those who seek You." Psalm 9:10 (ESV)

Action Steps:

- ✓ Seek with all your heart and you will find God.

- ✓ Look for new opportunities in your schedule to spend time with God through prayer, worship, and Scripture reading.

- ✓ Do not stop digging—you will never find all of God's treasure because it is endless.

- ✓ Journal everything that you discover and keep a record of the treasures God reveals to you.

CHAPTER 6

The Redesign

Are you ready to give God permission to redesign your life today? If so, come to the table with no preconceived ideas. He has made a way for you to come with a clean slate and a pure heart. Come hungry! Be willing to give up everything for His plan. Lay all your burdens at the feet of Jesus. Invite the Holy Spirit into every aspect of your life. God does not force His way on you, so in order to redesign your life, you must be willing to let go of the past.

Surrender, being willing to let go of the old thoughts and habits hindering your progress forward. Everything will shift for the ultimate good when you surrender to God's plan. God is the way-maker, but you must first give Him permission to lead the way. It is crucial to understand God's way does not look like the world's way. We see our earthly circumstances differently than God sees them. God's way is better, but it requires surrender and sacrifice. You need to make room for

Him to be the most important voice in your life. Come sit at His feet and learn. He is the master teacher. The Word of God is medicine—it has the power to heal! Repeat it daily. Use it as a weapon over your life. Do not allow the enemy to have a foothold. Stay vigilant!

One of the beautiful things about allowing God to redesign your life according to His plans is that He always has good ideas—just ask! Ask God for fresh manna, and He will provide. Ask God for your daily bread—for your portion. Ask God questions about your circumstances, like the management of your business or the rhythms of your daily life. Ask Him to reveal how His beautiful plan effects your everyday decisions. As you keep seeking, God will show up and answer those questions you have. The deeper you go with God, the more you will see through His eyes. Suddenly you will see with new eyes—the eyes of your heart. Taste and see that He is good.

Pray for an upgrade! "God, I want to know you in a deeper way. I am ready for an upgrade. I do not want to live this defeated life anymore. Sitting at your feet is where I feel safe. I surrender all to you—I am ready for the next best step, whatever that might look like! Give me eyes to see and ears to hear. I want to see with the eyes of my heart. Line up people in my life who will help me walk this new life out in You! You are the God of the new—the old is gone. The more I seek You, the more I want You, Father. Make me hungry for more of You. I want to drink from the cup in Your hand. In You is where I find my peace. Your love is so deep. I just want to know your heart and how it applies to my life. Father, let Thy will be done on earth as it is in Heaven. In Jesus' name I pray. Amen."

God is faithful, and everything He does is to help you, not harm you. You will have to step out in faith and trust He is changing things for good. As you do, He will birth new visions inside your heart and mind. He will bring change all around you. People and things that were toxic in your life will start to slowly disappear, but God will bring people into your life to help you walk this journey out. It does not always happen overnight, but your life *will* start to change, my friend. You will look back in a year and not believe who you have become.

I pray this book will spark a fire in you to want to know why you were created. We were all created for something greater, but it is only discovered by seeking the One who created you. He will give you lots of help along the way; trust in His plan! He will move mountains out of your way so that His glory will be discovered! He is the God of breakthrough and transformation. Step to the side and let Him have His way with your life today!

Action Steps:

- ✓ Allow God to Redesign your life today!

- ✓ Show up hungry!

- ✓ Start with a clean slate and clean heart.

- ✓ Ask God for fresh new ideas.

- ✓ God's word has healing powers—use it daily!

- ✓ Let this be the spark to a new life in Christ!

- ✓ Journal everything that you discover as God redesigns your life.

Endnotes

Dionne White, https://www.dionnewhiteart.com/

Matt Tommey, The Thriving Christian Artist—https://www.matttommeymentoring.com/

Tommy Walker, "When we worship, the invisible God is at work doing invisible and powerful things. We get realigned, refreshed, and refueled; we find unspeakable joy and indescribable peace. We discover the breakthrough strength of God, which enables us to walk in the truth, live in His presence and see Him fight our battles for us. It is how we can put the beauty of the Gospel on display, receive His many blessings and at the same time be a blessing to the world." https://tbctoronto.org/the-power-of-praise-and-worship/

Bishop T.D. Jakes "When you hold onto your history you do it at the expense of your destiny." https://www.huffpost.com/entry/bishop-jakes-oprah-lifeclass_n_3922739

Karen Wheaton, https://karenwheaton.com/

About the Author

At first glance, Wendy Bryant may seem like an ordinary person. She is a mother, a daughter, and a friend. But if you look again, you will see that Wendy has unlocked the secret of how to live an extraordinary existence in the midst of an ordinary life. Wendy's approach on how to redesign a life is simple, yet powerful. If you find yourself in need of a divine reset, this book is for you.

For the past eleven years, Wendy has been dressing the physical bodies of women all over the world. She also loves teaching others how to create their own wardrobe out of discarded clothing. Her passion is to help others recognize who they are in Christ. One way she is doing this is through an online community called "Creative Businesswomen of Faith."

Wendy gives back by helping the street children of Uganda, Africa. She has helped build an orphanage and continues to help with projects when needed.

Wendy is a South Louisiana native. She spent 18 years of her life in Memphis, Tennessee, but returned home to South Louisiana in 2007. She has three children Austin, Sean, and Hollie.

Contact or Invite Wendy to speak @ www.wendy-bryant.com or redesignyourlifebook@gmail.com. If you are interested in knowing more about "Creative Businesswomen of Faith" you can find information @ www.wendy-bryant.com.

www.ingramcontent.com/pod-product-compliance
Lightning Source LLC
Chambersburg PA
CBHW071518030726
47593CB00003B/1316